LIFE LESSONS FROM
YOUR DOG

IF DRINKING FROM
THE TOILET IS WRONG,
I DON'T WANT TO BE RIGHT

ANTHONY RUBINO JR.

THOMAS NELSON
Since 1798

NASHVILLE   DALLAS   MEXICO CITY   RIO DE JANEIRO   BEIJING

Published in Nashville, TN, by Thomas Nelson. Thomas Nelson is a trademark of Thomas Nelson, Inc.

Thomas Nelson, Inc., titles may be purchased in bulk for educational, business, fundraising, or sales promotional use. For information, please e-mail SpecialMarkets@ThomasNelson.com.

Illustrations by Anthony Rubino Jr.

Library of Congress Cataloging-in-Publication Data
Rubino, Anthony, 1966–
  Life lessons from your dog : if drinking from the toilet is wrong, I don't want to be right / Anthony Rubino, Jr.
      p. cm.
  ISBN-13: 978-1-4016-0343-4
  ISBN-10: 1-4016-0343-2
  1. Dogs—Humor. I. Title.
  PN6231.D68R83 2007
  818'.602—dc22

                                                                    2007007510

Printed in the United States of America
07 08 09 10 11 — 5 4 3 2 1

TO MY FATHER, who told my sisters and me
that he was allergic to dogs
so that he didn't have to get us one

AND TO MY MOTHER, who knew
he was lying but went along with it

SPECIAL THANKS

Special thanks go to Oreo, Elvis, Duncan, Lily, Kevin, Urcy, Kellie, and Tippie, and to those trick leashes that make it look like you're walking an invisible dog. Those things are funny for so many reasons. Not the least of which being that . . . well . . . you know . . . it looks like you're walking an invisible dog.

This book is in memory of Luigi the Hamster. I never got you that extra Habitrail tube I promised you before you died of a tiny little heart attack. Sorry, man. Oh . . . I'm also sorry I named you Luigi when actually you were a chick.

Thanks also to my editor, Jennifer Greenstein; and my agent, Jim McCarthy; and to Bryan Curtis for getting the party started.

My husband and I are either going to buy a dog or have a child. We can't decide whether to ruin our carpets or ruin our lives.
—RITA RUDNER

Outside of a dog, a book is probably man's best friend, and inside of a dog, it's too dark to read.
—GROUCHO MARX

Support your local ASPCA:
www.aspca.org

Adopt a dog:
www.americanhumane.org

Foster a dog: www.littleshelter.com

INTRODUCTION

So I'm on a hot date in the park with a gorgeous, dumb blonde when I experience an awkward moment. My date wouldn't give me back my stick. I tugged on it a few times until I realized that she was not letting it go because she was tired and just didn't want to play any more. The date I was having was with my dog, Lola.

"Hey, you're not as dumb as you look," I said, as I tussled her head and sat on the ground beside her. She happily dropped down on her haunches and we sprawled out on the grass.

Almost immediately my mind started to wander. I began thinking about the bills I had to pay, the work I had waiting for me at home, and the errands I had yet to complete. Before long I began to feel the all-too-familiar anxiety of my daily existence closing in around me like a vise. I turned to Lola for a commiserative look of understanding; instead I received a paw on my shoulder and a friendly wet lick. Lola felt no anxiety, of course. Lola was content just to be content.

"Content just to be content," I said out loud. "What must *that* be like?" And then it hit me. No, not the idea for this book—not yet. The stick I had been throwing hit me on the head because Lola had it in her jaws and was swinging it back and forth with *her* head. She was ready to play again, but I had some questions. And there in front of me were all the answers. Lola had the secret to happiness, and I was determined to get it from her. No, my dog was not as dumb as she looked. In fact, my dog was smarter than I was!

It was becoming all too clear that we humans are *not* the superior of the two species. Within the confines of the symbiotic dog/man relationship, humans are definitely getting the short end of this particular saliva-covered stick.

While Lola gnawed on her branch I thought, *Isn't it telling that while our dogs are content, we are confused and concerned? Where they are at peace, we are perturbed and perplexed. Dogs do pretty much whatever they feel like doing—whenever they feel like doing it—while we spend our lives doing things we'd rather not, pausing only long enough to assist our pooches in their effortless quest for happiness. Despite our large craniums and opposable thumbs, our dogs wind up getting the lion's share of the relationship deal.*

Armed with this new revelation that I was nowhere near as intelligent as a forty-two-pound quadrupedal canine with a brain the size of a tangerine, I was unburdened! I was free to turn to our dog brothers and sisters and ask for help. And that is exactly what I did.

I set out on a quest for dog knowledge. I traversed the globe, interviewing dogs along the way and observing canine behavior as I went. I embedded myself in the fuzzy folds of dog dogma, mining for rich nuggets of pooch philosophy. Yes—I became one with my inner wolf!

And here on the following pages are the fruits of my exhaustive labor, ready and waiting to be lapped up by all of mankind, like . . . well . . . like toilet water.

Pay close attention to the following kernels of kennel wisdom—they just might pave the path to happiness and contentment for you. Yes, friends, the cat no longer has the dog's tongue. Our precious pooches finally have a voice. And that voice resonates in this book: *Life Lessons from Your Dog*—an in-depth look at the advice our dogs would give to us if they could speak, as well as the advice they would give to their dog colleagues and peers.

So curl up by the fire with your favorite chew toy, turn the page, and embark (no pun intended) on a journey into the mind of your dog. Because it *is* a dog-eat-dog world after all and you need all the help you can get.

Life is short—pet hard.

A dog is man's best friend.
Cats are acquaintances at best.

A fool and his sandwich are soon parted.

Why won't they let you bite the delivery guy when clearly he's come to eat the children? Same reason they keep letting the vacuum cleaner out! Who the heck knows?

"Good dog." "Bad dog." Ya know . . . sometimes we just want to be an "OK dog" and leave it at that.

Furriness is next to godliness.

Cleanliness is next to . . . well, to be
honest, cleanliness is not a big priority.

Positive reinforcement is the best method of training. So when it looks like they're gonna give you a treat, do a trick. They seem to respond well to that.

I know you don't like it when I bark at the squirrels, but . . . um . . . *hello!* *You* spend all day peeing a perimeter around the yard, and see if you don't get cheesed off!

Gosh! We don't mean to gush. Maybe you did just go to get the mail, but in dog years you've been gone for . . . like a week!

Be careful what you wish for. Back in the summer of 2001 I actually *caught* my tail. And . . . I gotta tell ya . . . it wasn't that great.

Don't take people too literally. My person kept saying he wanted me to learn a new trick, but when I made the cat disappear he was not amused.

Starve a cold, feed a cold nose.

I'm in love with your left golf shoe.
There I said it! Now just leave us alone!

Dude, if I let go of the stick, you're just gonna throw it again! What's my motivation?

Can't sleep at night? Whine, bark, and scratch at the door. Then you'll have some company.

So I said, "I find you overbearing and self-absorbed, and frankly I think it's because you're just not comfortable in your own skin." And that was the last time he asked me to "speak."

Just ignore all those people who think dogs have it so easy. I mean, come on! It takes Zen-like concentration to take fourteen naps a day!

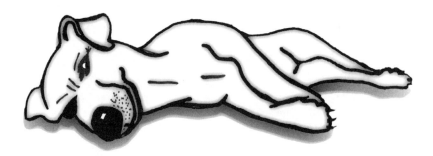

When you discover that your dog has chewed the furniture or broken something, take a deep breath and count to ten before you act.

When a person discovers that you've chewed the furniture or broken something, run away while they're counting to ten.

Exactly what part of *woof* don't you understand?

Always remember: home is where the heart is . . . and the liver and the kidneys and the snout and whatever else they put in dog food.

If you get nervous around those high-class city dogs, sometimes it helps to picture them without their sweaters on.

Focus with extreme and laser-like intensity on the task at hand until a shiny object or a chipmunk distracts you. Then abandon what you're doing and focus with extreme and laser-like intensity on that.

Outside is great. Unless you *are* outside. In which case inside is the place to be . . . but that's soooo boring! So . . . outside is where the action is, but it's cold out there . . . so you'll want to be back inside so you can start thinking about how great it would be to be outside again.

Don't be concerned that you only
have one name . . . works for Cher.

People can be so selfish. I mean, you put your head right on their lap, so that it's super-convenient for them to stop what they're doing and pet you—and they act like you're not doing them a favor.

23

Do it on the lawn.

They say a dog's mouth is cleaner than a human's. That's just not #@%! true.

Hey. Thanks for throwing that tennis ball over and over. Seriously, man, you wouldn't catch me picking up that thing with all that spit on it.

Bark first. Ask questions later.
Then go ahead and bark again.

If I've gotta wait outside that deli tied
to a tree, you better be walkin' outta
there with some vinegar and onion
potato chips, missy!

Don't bother us with trivial matters
when we're in the throes of calamity!
Can't you see that my ball just rolled
under the couch?! This is a *disaster!*

DOe$GS SH!dfOULD NknjEVER #TYPE
THIE2%R OWN MANUxe$SCRIPTS.

Today: Take a nap, run around the yard really fast, lick your privates, stretch, yawn, take a longer nap, bark at the UPS guy.

Tomorrow: Take a nap, lick your privates, *then* run around the yard really fast, stretch, yawn, take a longer nap, bark at the UPS guy. You know . . . mix it up a little.

Practice random acts of mayhem.

If you have to throw up, do it on a chair or a couch. You don't want to be stepping in that nasty stuff later on.

Put yourself in our place for a moment. Now think what it must be like—what with being on all fours and not having opposable thumbs—and maybe you'll start to understand that we, once again, find ourselves in the rather awkward position of asking you for another cookie.

What?! Like you wouldn't lick yourself there if you could?

If a lamp falls in the living room and there is no one there to hear it—blame the cat.

You may think we stay out of trouble when we're asleep. But sister, we're dreamin' up all manner of funky stuff to do when we wake up. *You have no idea.*

Chocolate is very bad for dogs. Lethal even! Boy, I learned that the hard way—five times—last week.

No use cryin' over spilt milk—or spilt anything for that matter. It's *much* easier to get to it that way.

Work very hard at resting.

Stay away from Korean restaurants.
Just trust me on this.

If I'm takin' a bath . . . everybody's takin' a bath.

When we're walking down the street together and we pass another dog, just let me smell that dog. Do I stop you from waving to *your* friends?

Rules are like garbage cans. You don't know what you're dealing with until you knock 'em over and root through their contents.

Respect children and the elderly.
Both are very likely to drop food.

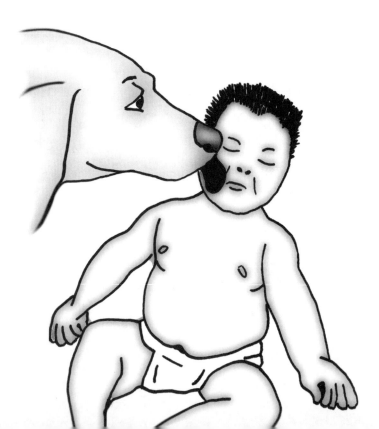

You know how sometimes a person
will tell you to "stay" and you do—
but you were gonna stay anyway?
Yeah . . . ya gotta love that.

Don't be fooled. Real bones rarely squeak.

Retrievers retrieve. Pointers point. And shih tzus . . . are excellent watchdogs. What? *They are!*

I could be barking at a prison escapee outside, hiding in wait. I could be barking at a branch. Good luck with that!

Oh . . . we'll eat the hunk of ground beef with the pill in it. But you're not foolin' anybody.

People make a big fuss when you sprawl out on your back and stick your private parts in the air. Well, if you can think of a better way to air out your genitals, I'd like to hear it.

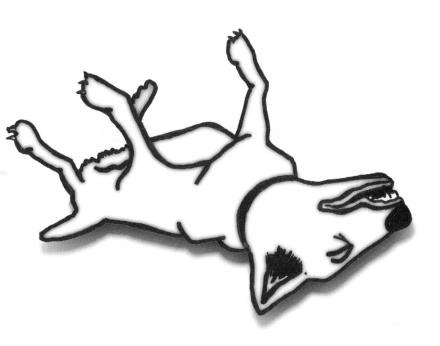

Pretending you don't hear your person is more reliable than the "mistaken identity tactic." It's difficult to act like they're talking to someone else when you're the only Attila in the house.

Four out of five female dogs
fake wagging.

Don't expect us to fetch.
Just be happy when we do.

All work and no play makes you
a . . . well . . . a human.

Dogs may seem needy and stupid, but that's only because we're so clingy and dumb.

You got it, so flaunt it. There's nothing wrong with shaking your tail every now and then to get your way.

Make full eye contact when you want something. Make full body contact if you don't get it.

A dog's age isn't what it used to be. They say that these days "your age times seven" is the new "your age times six."

People are hypocrites. Some of the same women who don't use choke collars because they're "cruel" are dressing us in sweaters and carrying us around in purses!

Be true to your drool.

I don't roll over for just anybody.
They have to have some food.

You know we're just messing with
you when we're playing catch and
we won't give you the ball back, right?
Kind-a like when you pretend to throw
it and we go running after nothing.
Touché, my friend, touché!

Lick others often and without warning.

Speak in high-pitched friendly tones
when you want your dog to obey.
It won't do you any good, but it's
entertaining.

Scratch anywhere—any time.

Having a cat as a pet is like having a shar-pei with a facelift. *What's the point?*

Smarty, Skippy, Rex, Rover, Spot, Belvedere, Mr. Flaps, Precious, Mercedes, Beamer, Oreo, Tinkles, Dinky, Thor, Zeus (pagan gods in general), Lassie, Yeller, Clifford, Mr. Moo Cow (Mr. *Anything* really), FiFi, Farah, Poo, and Tigger. Yeah . . . don't name us that.

Remember, "dog eat dog" is an expression—not a suggestion.

Don't overdo it. Just because you've got six nipples doesn't mean you have to have a half-a-dozen kids. Some of those can be spares, ya know.

Listen, I'm not telling you how to run things, but I for one wouldn't be so quick to just accept that it's OK for the cat to be away. I mean who's gotta pick up the slack for the mice being at play? The *dog*—that's who!

Of course we look up to you.
We're only as tall as your knee.

There's no such thing as a free puppy.

Nothing says "I love you"
like a freshly killed possum.

63

People have screwed-up priorities.
They say stuff like, "If you're not
careful the world will pass you by."
Like that's a *bad* thing?

Fur is murder—on chenille.

There's always time for a quickie.
Naps! I'm talkin' about naps!

It's hard to think about, but you really need to get your affairs in order and draw up a will. You know, so the little details don't get overlooked—stuff like where you want to be laid to rest, the type of service you want, whether to leave your estate to your rotten kids who never visit and don't deserve a cent, or to . . . oh . . . I don't know . . . a beloved pet who's not the cat. That sort of thing.

It's important to be vigilant and alert at all times—or you might miss that ideal napping spot.

Please . . . just go ahead and curse already. "Doggone it" is just way too easily misunderstood.

How was I supposed to know you were only going to the bathroom? You close that door and for all I know you've stepped into another freakin' dimension! I mean . . . my brain is the size of a tangerine, for cryin' out loud!

Who are you kidding? All dogs are "lap dogs."

Have you ever woken up and thought it was the weekend, but it turned out to be a weekday and you had to go to work? Yeah . . . there's no life lesson here, I'm just sayin' . . . that must suck for you.

Here we are now. Entertain us.

It's OK to chase chipmunks
up until the third trimester.

Going to the park without a ball is like eating bubbles. It's pointless and it leaves a bad taste in your mouth.

People remedies don't always work on dogs. For example, when shelties can't sleep, counting sheep just totally stresses them out.

There is an anti-dog conspiracy. I won't say who's behind it, but when was the last time you saw a "No Cats Allowed" sign? Think about it.

If you don't want to get in trouble, just don't jump on the guests. I mean, come on! It's not doorknob science!

It's good to be the dog.

When in doubt, scratch something
extremely personal.

Sure I want you to pay attention to me all the time. But I know you need romance in your life. And when you find that special someone I'll be cool with that—because then you can *both* pay attention to me all the time.

When someone tells you to "get down" they probably want you to get off of a piece of furniture or countertop. It rarely means you should get up and start dancing.

With a well-timed whine, you will dine.

They watch you go to the bathroom.
You watch them go to the bathroom.
It's disturbing, but fair.

Sit. Stay. Come. Heel. Honestly, it gets a little old. How about "How was your day?" once in a while?

If you don't have to lie down to scratch your belly on the carpet, you may be workin' on a weight problem there, Fido.

Being a dog takes a certain amount of humility, but it's all a matter of perspective. So when people start to get a little too superior, just remind yourself who is picking up whose poop.

Don't corner hard on tile.

How do you spell relief?
E-A-T-G-R-A-S-S.

If it looks like a duck and acts like a duck, but it smells like rubber and squeaks . . . watch your back, man, 'cus you-know-who might be getting ready to give you a bath.

Oh, you can circle around that spot on the floor two times instead of three before you lie down. But do you really want to take that chance? *Do you?*

Save that last bite of food for later. Yeah . . . while you're at it, get up on your hind legs and sing Pagliacci . . . I'm just messing with you!

Quench your need for speed. And if you wind up getting a bug in your mouth . . . hey . . . bonus!

Too much of a good thing
is a better thing.

Beware of the vet.
Goin' for a ride—my ass!

People want you to heel, go to the bathroom outdoors, and stay off the furniture. So go easy on them. Their lives are filled with disappointment.

Don't be intimidated by those hoity-toity full breeds who think they're all that. They lift one leg at a time when they pee, just like everybody else.

People make a big fuss when you roll around in the mud. Well, if you can think of a better way to get mud all over you, I'd like to hear it!

TV dogs are unstable. Just look at Lassie. She obviously had some serious emotional problems because they were always telling her to "get help."

The grass is always greener on the other side of the fence because those people don't have a dog.

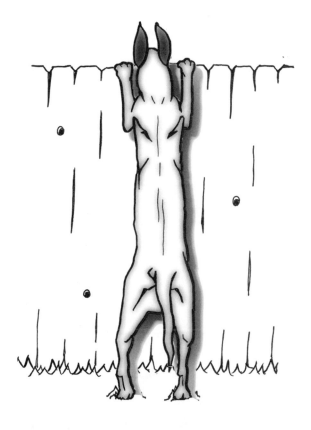

What's the puzzle? We like to nuzzle.

If you can't be with the one you love,
breed with the one you're with.

LAWS OF DOG PHYSICS

An object in perpetual motion tends
to stay in motion. An object at
perpetual rest tends to be a dog.

A dog at rest tends to stay at rest
unless acted upon by your saying
something that sounds like "park."

The distance between where you're tied up
and the curb decreases exponentially by
the amount of times you wrap your chain
around the lawn chair. Stupid lawn chair!

The height of the counter decreases
proportionately by the amount of
sausage that is left on it to defrost.

As a rule, don't let drool pool.

Do your part to make guests feel welcome by accompanying them into the bathroom. You don't have to do anything. Just sit there and stare at them while they relieve themselves.

Sure, people get upset when you wake them up. But don't blame yourself! It's not *your* fault they're so boring when they're asleep.

Hey, we don't mean to seem ungrateful. We know you mean well . . . and that you're just trying to help. But the little booties are really just not necessary.

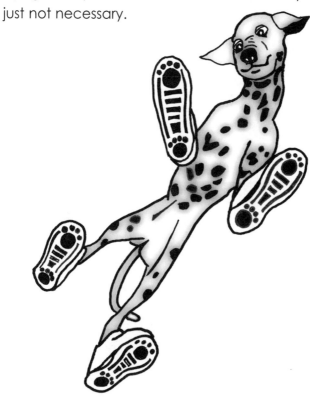

The truth shall set you flea.

Have respect for all the creatures on
the earth—that can run faster than you.

Dog toys are great, but I'm just as happy with a ball or a stick. I mean . . . I need another squeaky toy like you need another dog book.

Curiosity killed the cat, officer.
I was at my girlfriend's house all night.

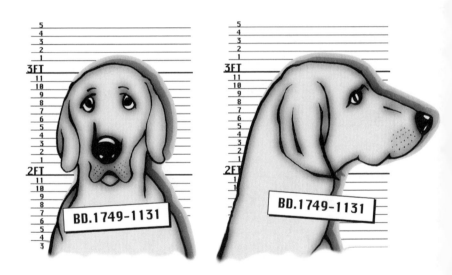

Don't take our frequent whining to mean we're needy. We're pretty much needy whether we whine or not.

You know what you call a place with two off-white rugs and an expensive oriental carpet?
A three-bathroom home.

Dogs may have short attention spans,
but at least we . . . Ooh! Squirrel!

Yes, I know I shouldn't have taken everything out of the pantry and chewed it, but *for goodness sake*— I couldn't help myself! Don't you know a cry for help when you see one?!

People don't like it when you bark at the paperboy. But it's like "Look . . . I'm territorial! I'm a pack animal. You knew that going into this relationship."

Hiding under the blanket is only a temporary fix.

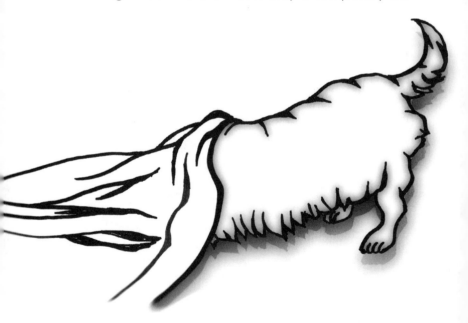

Don't get caught up in whether
you're a "mixed breed" or "full breed,"
like some people do. Who died and
made *them* "Best in Show"?

If you love something, set it free. If it comes back, it's yours. If it doesn't come back, bark and bark and then bark and bark and just bark and bark and bark and bark and bark . . .

Let's see how good an idea you think the Hannibal Lecter muzzle is when that guy with the weird hair tries to talk to you again.

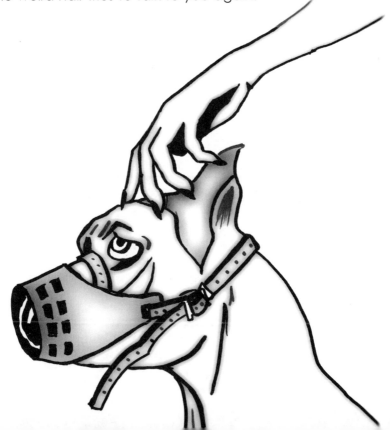

You are only as old
as you feel—times seven.

If the leg's a-thwappin',
don't let 'em stop a-scratchin'!

Next time you get yelled at for no good reason, let it go. People have bad days too. It's not as easy as it looks to walk upright and act like you're in charge of the planet.

Consider not neutering.
Puppies make great holiday gifts!

Be proud. Say what you want about all our bad habits, but at least we've got our integrity. You don't see us blaming people in the room when we fart.

People are mystified by the oddest things—like how we always know exactly when to wait at the door for our owner to come home from work. Duh! She comes home at five thirty every day.

Don't be afraid to jerk on that leash when
they're not going where you want them to.
You won't hurt them.

Never put off until later the nap
you could be taking right now.

Be politically correct. Remember,
it's "mixed breed" not "mutt."

Never "play dead" if your owner is a mortician. I knew a spaniel who was showin' off one-day—brother was six feet under before he ever got to his big "roll over" finish.

Watch for subtle hints
that your dog wants to go out.

Fish gotta swim, birds gotta fly.
If you leave the pantry open,
kiss the cookies goodbye.

I promise to love, honor, and yes, obey you in sickness and in health till death do us part. You may nuzzle the hound.

If God had wanted us to be neat, he would have made us cats.

People say, "You are what you eat."
Oh man, I hope not.

Isn't it amazing when you see a headline that reads something like "Dog Finds His Way Home: Travels 300 Miles to Owner's Doorstep after Six Months"? Yeah, how 'bout "Stupid Owner Leaves Dog on Side of Highway: Travels 300 Miles Without Noticing—Like an Idiot!" Talk about burying the lead!

We're here! We're nonpedigree!
Get used to it!

Nothing says love like collecting a
sample of our poop to show the vet.

The right collar can be quite slimming.

Don't play favorites. Love the cable guy as deeply and passionately as you love the person who has fed and cared for you every day for a decade.

If you are jumpy, hyperactive, paranoid, overly sensitive, unconcerned about personal hygiene, and willing to abandon all semblance of dignity and self-respect, you may be addicted to crack . . . then again, you may be a dog.

Remember, it's only *his*
favorite chair when he's home.

One good turn gets most of the covers.

Appreciate your people. That kind of unconditional love is hard to find.

Berber carpets make pretty good
butt scratchers. Persian rugs will do
in a pinch if the pile is deep enough.
But shag! Oh Lord . . . shag is just a
little slice of heaven.

A watched ice cream cone never drips.

If you'd just get furniture, carpeting, and drapes that matched your dog's fur, then the shedding wouldn't be a problem now, would it?

Careful. It's all too easy to let that chew toy become a crutch.

Guard dogs guard. Attack dogs attack. Watch dogs watch. Hot dogs . . . *mmmmmmm* . . . hoooooot dooooooogs . . .

I may be nothing but a hound dog, and sure, maybe I never caught a rabbit. But to say I'm no friend of yours . . . that's just hurtful.

Biscuit:
One sit and a paw on command.

Table scrap:
Five minutes of staring
and three whimpers.

A dinner plate left on the coffee table:
Priceless.

Heel. Stay. Come. Sit. Fetch. Shake. Lie. Jump.
Beg. And you wonder why I chew the cushions?

If dogs could talk we'd want to
know the answer to some pretty
deep questions. Like "What happens
to you in the 'great beyond'?"
You know . . . when you go into the
bathroom and close the door.

Staring is rude? *Really?* And what is eating the best parts of a delicious, ground-up, hoofed animal between two tasty buns—in front of an instinctual carnivore with extremely sensitive olfactory glands? Polite?!

It's not that we want you to be home all the time. It's just that when you're not we feel like our little heads are gonna explode!

Yeah . . . uh huh! You're not gonna lock me in the laundry room? No . . . you just want to show me something in there, right? Is that your story? Sure, and Champ went to a big farm in the country where he can *run* and *run* all day long. *Do I look like I was born yesterday?*

Where there's a will, there's a way to get your head into a mayonnaise jar.

Oh please! Spare me the lies! I can smell that other dog all over you!

It's strange that people are amazed at our ability
to "enjoy the moment." What else is there?

If people are so smart, how come they haven't figured out a way to lick their own privates?

Many of us haven't had our "day" yet. But it's nice to have something to look forward to.

"Beware of dog" is such a broad
statement. Consider elaborating.
Ya know, maybe "Beware of dog
because he's had a rough week."
Or "Beware of dog—she's a little skittish
since the 'meter-reader incident.'"
It's nice to be understood.

You can tell a lotta lies when
you flash those puppy dog eyes.

Chase cars all you want—just don't catch one. 'Cus then you'll be all . . . "OK, *now* what?"

Appreciate your people. I mean, *come on!* What other species is gonna let us get away with the stuff we do?!

Thou shalt have no other pets before me.

ABOUT ANTHONY RUBINO JR

Tony was raised by a pack of wild poodles until he was ostracized for making an off-color remark about the French. An Italian family in New Jersey felt sorry for the young dog-boy and took him in. But once again he found himself on the street shortly after refusing a second helping of pasta fagioli. Fortunately, by then he was thirty-five.

Shunned by both dog and human societies, Tony began to look inward and embarked on a quest for knowledge through the careful study of drivel. Never a stickler for math, Tony wrote *Life Lessons from Your Dog* as the fifth installment of his Life-Lessons trilogy, which includes *Life Lessons from Your Cat, Life Lessons from Elvis, Life Lessons from the Bradys,* and *Life Lessons from Melrose Place.* He began his scholarly pursuits by penning *1001 Reasons to Procrastinate.* He's also contributed articles and cartoons to publications such as *MAD Magazine, National Lampoon,* the *Chicago Tribune,* and *Opium Magazine.*

His cartoon syndication credits include national distribution by King Features, Tribune Media Services, and Creators Syndicate.

Tony's designs, cartoons, and words can be found on greeting cards and other product lines such as calendars, posters, and apparel sold in stores and catalogs worldwide.

When he's not goofing off with that stuff, you can find him living and working in New York City as a creative director and art director for the advertising and marketing industry—or watching TV.

Despite his repeated attempts to reconcile with his families, they continue to refuse his letters. He suspects it's because the poodles can't read and the Italians hold grudges. Or vice versa.

Visit www.rubinocreative.com for more information and big fun.